Matisse

King of Colour

LAURENCE ANHOLT

F

FRANCES LINCOLN
CHILDREN'S BOOKS

Monique climbed the steep hill

and up some long steps
to a huge building high
above the town.

The sign by
the door said:

Henri Matisse

It was like stepping into a multi-coloured jungle!

Birds flew from room to room and plants grew tall as trees.

"Hello," called a small voice, "is that the night nurse?"

"Hello, Mr Matisse," said Monique. "I have come to look after you."

The old artist had a silver beard and twinkly glasses. He was recovering from a big operation. The doctors thought he would never paint again.

"I feel a little better," he said, "but I would like you to read to me."

So Monique chose a book. She read for a long time.
Matisse didn't sleep...
but Monique did!

"Oh! I'm sorry," she said. "This is my very first job."

Matisse just smiled. "Look. I made a drawing of you."

Then Matisse told her about his adventures in different lands...

diving in tropical lagoons and rowing on blue-green seas.

And soon Monique forgot it was night outside.

Matisse loved music.

Matisse loved flowers.

Matisse loved children too.

He tied chalk to
a long stick so that he could draw
his grandchildren on the ceiling.

"They keep me company
when I can't sleep,"
he said.

But the thing Matisse loved most of all was...

COLOUR

He was always trying to find ways to make his paintings brighter and brighter. Some people called him the Wild Beast because his colours were so crazy.

Every evening, Monique climbed the hill to the
jungle studio. Monique helped Matisse to sit up
and paint and they became good friends.

Matisse made lots of pictures of Monique...

*in a beautiful
silk dress...*

with a mandolin on a chair.

And all his work was full of joy.

"There's enough sadness in the world," he would say.

"Look how much better I am," said Matisse one day. "It's like having a new life! Thank you for looking after me, Monique."

"You have been like a grandfather to me," said Monique.

Then Monique picked up her bag and walked slowly out of the jungle room. She thought she would never see Matisse again.

Monique went to school
far away in the mountains.

But it was not an ordinary school. Everybody dressed in black and white.
There were no colours at all. Monique's school was a school for nuns.

Life was very hard and the nuns were so poor, they didn't even have a
proper chapel... they had to say their prayers in a cold, leaky garage.

When the old nuns heard that Monique had been a nurse, they gave her a bicycle and sent her to look after people who weren't well. Every day Monique cycled along the lane, past a big empty house. The house had views right across the mountains to the sea. It was called 'The Dream'.

One afternoon in June, Monique saw that a new owner was moving into The Dream.
The new owner loved birds. The new owner loved cats.
The new owner was...

Henri Matisse

Matisse was delighted
to see Monique again.
"You are all black and white,"
he teased, "but I have
found a way to be more
colourful than ever!

Look, I'll show you…

First I put on some music. Jazz is best.

Now I paint some big sheets of paper…
as BRIGHT as I can!"

Then, with hands as quick as butterflies, Matisse cut
a hundred dancing shapes, and soon they were pinned up
on every wall of The Dream.

"I have been painting too," said Monique shyly. She showed Matisse a tiny picture. It was a design for a stained glass window.

"We could have this made with real stained glass – as high as this room!" said Matisse.

But Monique laughed. "The nuns don't even have a chapel – You can't put stained glass windows in a garage!"

It was nearly dark when Monique ran home. The nuns would be cross... and look, Monique was covered in splashes of colour!

"Come back soon!" laughed Matisse. Late into the night, the lights burned at The Dream.

Matisse was working on an idea!

Next time Monique called, she found Matisse very excited.

"Monique, you have been so kind to me. This is my idea...
I am going to build a chapel up here in the mountains –
not a dark, gloomy church. My chapel will be a house of colour!
It will be my present for you."

Matisse asked Monique to build a model
like a big doll's house.

"Now all I have to do is fill your box
with my imagination!"

Matisse made wonderful drawings for the chapel walls; he even designed some colourful robes for the priests to wear!

"We do not want a chapel built by a Wild Beast," grumbled the old nuns.

The chapel took a very long time. Matisse became tired; he asked the carpenter to put wheels on a bed and a tray for his paints. Matisse called it his Taxi-Bed!

At last the workmen began to put
up the chapel walls. Their bangs and
shouts echoed through the mountains.

The chapel had a bright blue roof
and a golden bell on a curly tower.

"This will be more like a circus than
a chapel," said the old nuns.

Monique was surprised. Everything seemed to be shiny white –
it didn't look like a house of colour at all! Perhaps the nuns had won.
The chapel was black and white, just like their clothes.

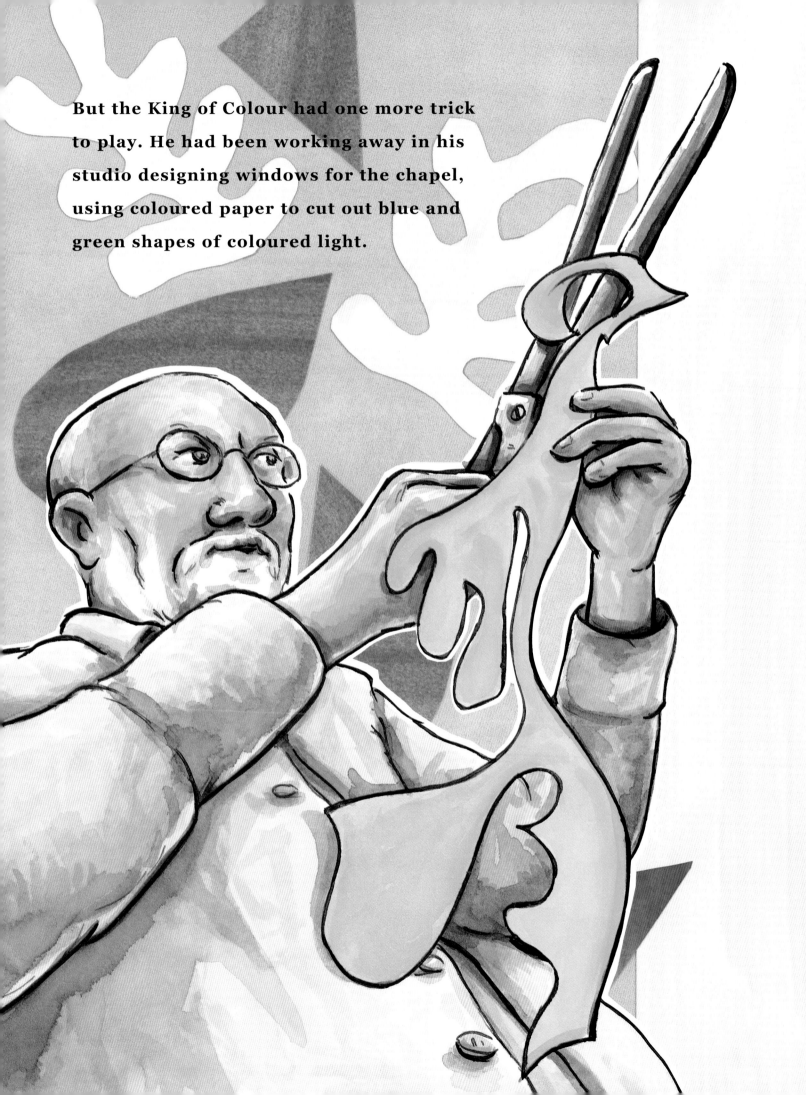

But the King of Colour had one more trick to play. He had been working away in his studio designing windows for the chapel, using coloured paper to cut out blue and green shapes of coloured light.

Seventeen stained glass windows were made
in a factory exactly as Matisse had planned.
A big truck climbed slowly up the mountain
and the workmen lifted them carefully in place.

Then they
drove back down
the mountain
and the chapel
was finished.

Then something amazing happened…

...the morning sun rose over the mountains and a bright ray of sunlight fell across the darkened windows.

Very slowly, the room began to fill with coloured light. It crept across the floor and on to the white walls.

Then, just like a magic painting book, the black and white world filled with beautiful colours.

Monique felt as if she was floating in a multi-coloured sea.

Matisse was painting with light!

Monique stood for a moment.

Then she went to wake the others.

High on the blue roof, the golden bell began to chime.

It echoed across the mountains to the sea.

As the sunlight
filled his bedroom,
Matisse heard
the sound,
and he smiled.

"Now I can rest,"
said the
King of Colour.